motherload

# motherload

by

suzanne rae deshchidn, mfa, ma, lsw

Raven Croaks Publishing

Raven Croaks Publishing San Bernardino

Editor Murray Pura
Interior design by Ron Brauer
Cover Photo by Analia Martinez ©2022 used by permission

www.ravencroaks.com

*for jackie, my gorgon*
*whose pronouns are they, them, theirs*

*i love thee knee*
*and thy vermicious knid,*
*zagreus, and charon too*

# table of contents

## step one

i quit the twelve step program    because i couldn't
admit i was powerless    i couldn't admit i wanted
control    even the hot lesbian    i gave my number to
couldn't convince me    i was powerless
        *i've worked too long and hard to own    my power*
i told her    over coffee    *i will admit to misapplying*
*my power    even giving it away    but never    to*
*being    powerless*
she laughed    in her own manic way    but today
today i would have struck a deal    with anyone
between classes    during my only break    i get a
frantic call    and a text    from my best friend
stranded on the gw bridge    *help*    the text read
she'd been in an accident    poor thing    she's a
magnet for bad drivers    this time    her car is likely
totaled    she's already got a metal plate    in her
neck from the first time someone rear ended her
now she's sitting on the bridge crying    it's the week
before finals    i have forty students yet to see    it's
my long day    i know there will be questions    i
can't abandon them    so i call    everyone i can
think of    my ex does not answer    my new friend
is at work    my neighbor obliges    but says
        *it's a historic moment    i'm watching    the shuttle*
*on channel two*    he doesn't want to    drive the hour
round trip to retrieve her

1

i am in classes until two thirty     calling     texting
it amounts to little    i get word
     *they're towing me*
     *i will be there as soon as i can*
my students     watch as i try to keep moving
forward    fielding calls and texts during class     so
unlike me   but i can just imagine her     stranded     so
i let them go    as quickly as possible     though i'm
only out of class     fifteen minutes earlier it's the week
before finals     they had questions i had to answer
driving to where i think she is as fast as i possibly can
she calls
     *where are you*
     *home*     she says
     *no way*    *i  am on my way to get you*
     *no*     she says
i turn my car around     and sit in rush hour traffic
for the first time    in a long time     i feel  powerless
i understand     i have no control

## half woman

how does half
   a woman
fashion   a whole
   life   where
does she begin
   how many
times i've tried
   to fulfill my
dreams   but that
   is the way
i guess   to keep
   a whole woman
half   i wondered
   some time ago
what i would do
   if you were gone
and i had to make a
   life   how it would
look   just as i wonder
   that now   i came
to you with a little
   i leave with   little
more   but how does
   a woman begin a
new life   beholden
   to none   cowering

behind    no man    finding
    a way to make
ends meet      the remnants
    of dreams    come
together    how does a
    half woman    become
whole again

## a young bride

we had only been married    eight weeks
and i had become    gravely ill    unable to
shake the haunt    that stole my breath away

watching roaches    crawl across the floor
and die    *don't unpack*    you said    we had
just begun    our nomadic life together

how i wanted to be in one place    forever
you came to california    and carried me
away    from family and friends    i took

you away    from the medicine road    you
walked with your aunt    she and i crossed
paths    the year before    at a powwow    she

your cousin's mother    i adored him and
danced with him often    i was no threat
to her then    until you    came along

though i swore    in that meeting    to have nothing
to do with her    ever    my will    would not prevail
she never uttered    a kind word to me

crouched low at her fireplace    indian housing on
the reservation     she chanted and cast her spell
striking me with an illness     she hoped

would free you    until you    dreamer    prophet
husband    saw her    and her spell was broken
        *i found out*    was all you would say

there was no medicine    that could cure me
other than your great love    and i arose from
six week's sickness    to see    another day

## bury me in the lake

*i want to be buried in the lake with my grandfathers*
you told me    as we drove across your reservation
up the mountains    into the forest    deep    where no
one    could find us    i saw the sign on the road
but you didn't    we kept driving    we were on sheer

cliffs    dropping thousands of feet    *we'll be alright*
you said    *as long as we don't hit snow*    our baby
riding in the car seat behind us    as we drove down
a one lane    dirt road    lined with pines    and in
the shade    around the bend    snow    you tried to

back up    but the dodge    had no traction    and
began to fishtail    with no room to maneuver    i
jumped out of the cab    stood at the sheer drop off
you pulled to the edge    and i told you to stop
the truck bumper    hit the mountainside    as you

backed as far as you could    we continued this
until inch    by nerve wracking inch    you turned
the truck around    what would i have done    if
you drove off the edge of the cliff    alone    in the
forest    with nothing    i imagined myself jumping

after you    and our baby    meeting you in the
cloud    of gasses and debris    where we would
live    with your ancestors    forever    today
so far from your people    and mine    i remember
those words    how i wanted to be with you then

and wonder where did it all go    did i jump off
that cliff with you    are we still there    with your
ancestors    will i someday    find myself    at the
bottom of the lake    with you and your people
or am i at the place    where i need to    send you
on your way    and set off    on mine

## twenty four hour wife

*try to act like a wife*
he said     i got that puzzled

what the hell     does that mean look
i've been thinking about it all day

and here's what i've come up with
if he means     june cleaver

i don't even own a dress     like that
i don't wear shoes     most days

when i do     they're flip flops
but i might manage it     if someone

wrote my lines     and paid me
and i got to go home after a half hour

all problems     resolved     that damned
smile on my face     but i'm a twenty

four hour wife     like lorraina bobbit
i spend entire days     hoofing it up and down

four flights of stairs     doing laundry
sweeping floors     cooking meals

educating our child
i endured four long years      of unemployment

and never once said
*act    like a husband*

though i did once say     *get a job*
i was tired      what can i say

sylvia plath      now there's another wife
maybe that's      what he means

## step two

*came to believe that a power greater than ourselves*
*could restore us to sanity.*

                    alcoholics anonymous

sometimes i agree    my sanity needs    restoration
like the chevy apache    parked    in my texas garage
the higher power    often feels as arbitrary as a
mechanic    his good days    a savior rescuing me
from beside the road    his bad failing to secure
connections    between electrical circuits    forcing
me to return    to his shop maybe that's the goal of
deities    to keep us coming back

but i've such a vast array    of alliances    quan yin
kali    sandalphon    ganesh    mary    christ    who
knows if they all get along    or want to    does this
make me insane    that i cannot ally myself    with
one    faith tradition    but find myself    making
peace    with all offering as much    respect to the
hindu pantheon    as any other

though it seems right to me    aslan
stretching out    his tongue    receiving
all devotion    as unto    himself

## the last fight

have you ever seen a woman
go flying     off the back
hand     of a man

the way my mother flew     the
length     of the king size bed
curlers flying     when she hit

the headboard
we walked in     just in time     to see it
screaming     and weeping

it was the last time     i saw my father cry
the last time     we lived together
as a family

we flit     like wounded birds     from bush
to bush     seeking refuge     my mother
carried a knife     on her daily run

she guarded us fiercely
until the lawyer advised her
to give us up
        *he'll keep them for six months*
        *then you'll have them back*

we never lived with my mother
again     it was no great torment
for me     a father's daughter

but my sister died that day     parted
from the one she knew since birth
given     to the one     who hated women

## sangre de dios

i pass the line of migrant workers     whose dark oval
faces     black hair     almond eyes     are the faces of all
those i have ever loved     those faces     not so much
hopeful     as determined mama     back at home
flips the tortilla dough     between her hands
singing     *ese lunar     que tienes cielito lindo     junto a la
boca*     the flat tortilla pan     and white linen towel
used for pressing     the dough on the fire     the
slender figure of the worker     trained not to eat too
much     until he gets home     to mama's comida
paid too little     for grueling work     standing in the
sun all day     waiting     endlessly waiting     the
children dressed     in cotton summer dresses     worn
thin from too much washing     if laughter were wages
we would be kings     mama is the world     and when
papa comes home     having drunk his wages     at the
bar with his buddies     she paints his toenails pink
as he's passed out     in the living room     a rookie cop
beats him for a fag     when he sees the nails     papa
never mentions it     but we know the story     i
remember it     every time     i drive past     the workers

## the karmic load

there is a fine line    between trust    and the willing of
fate to turn    in your favor    manifestation    is it the
same as prayer    is it the same    as trusting the
divine    to arbitrate    in your favor    because come
on    that is what we want    right

i have used worry    to remind myself    to ground
to state    how grateful i am    for everything    in my
life    from the people    i love    to my job    to what
my dog gobbled up in the yard    before i got to her
there seemingly    is no end    to the perceived

terror    that can befall a soul    or loved ones    and i
begin to wonder    how i can claim    any kind of
strength    when    i feel    this fragile    when my
mind whirrs    with the dizzying    details    of what
can    and arguably    should    go wrong

is my karmic load    that bad    or am i just afraid
that it might be    that i    have some    debt to pay
which at this point doesn't even appear to be mine
but hell    i'm a woman    a minority    i know how
to bear a burden    silently    but i want    to do more

than that   with what is left   of this life   so many
years   spent in wonder   in awe of all that is   and
could be   now here   in my years of fulfillment   i
buckle   at the thought   toss and turn   at the idea
that it could all   go horribly   wrong

what happened to the woman   who used to believe
it could all   go horribly right   where is she now
that my teeth are rebelling   and my bills unending
where is she now   her strength of will   and
undying belief   that it will all   work out

## six armed mother

    the twelve arms    of the two
        six armed woman and
        her six armed    gorgon
        synchronize in pool
one high    then low
        the two move    together
        laughing    giggling
        while mother
swims low    deep    near
        the bottom    and smiles
        at the sounds
        echoing    through the water
the trick    it seems    is to teach them
        how to move    with strength
        and certainty    how to fight
        with ferocity
without putting out    an eye
        with your own sword
        six arms    flailing
        elegantly

## calle muerto

traveling down highway 191    weary from an
impromptu road trip    with our ten week old
baby    buying pottery at pueblos    not the shiny
evenly shaped stuff    white people collect    but
the stuff    tribal people have in their homes
we went to their homes    and bought from them
pueblo after pueblo    zuni    isleta    acoma
santo domingo    taos    leaving with pots    and
arms full    of bread and fruit    we paid well
for misshapen earth    and were pleased    i am
still pleased    with my    not    museum worthy
collection    of pottery

leaving four corners    after the requisite shots
photos taken in each state    driving down the road
i am navigating from the back seat    but it's a
straight shot home    so i try to nod off    until i see
them    the first few    were no surprise    how
many exoduses    have been made to the sides of
roads    to leave descansos    recuerdos of a life
ended    mementos all    of love and loss    but they
would not    stop    coming

white wooden crosses    a hundred sixteen    when i
asked    *are you seeing this*    my eyes wide as saucers
        *yes*    he said    his eyes riveted to the road

death road    i call it now    we talked    the uneasy
talk    of travelers    trying to keep each other's
minds off    the grim realities    and inherent dangers
of travel    we talked in short quips    never big on
words    we held vigil together    hoping    not
to become    three more descansos    poquito
mediano    grande

we drove all night    past flagstaff    through phoenix
and pulled safely    into our chandler garage    piled
into bed    and slept    grateful    to be home again
at last

## step three

*made a decision to turn our will and our lives over*
*to the care of god as we understood him.*
alcoholics anonymous

let's start    with the obvious    masculine pronoun
i have resolved    my daddy issues    my ex husband
and i    have an amicable relationship    centered
appropriately    around    our gorgon    the only
other male in my life    is in the throes    of hormonal
change    in every way    my opposite    and ally
as i am of    that certain age    when summer
arrives unexpectedly    and lasts    for about five
minutes    just long enough    for me to strip down
to the barest lining    and chill    when the actual
winter temp    is felt    i have worked    long and hard
to reconcile    with christ energy    because i at least
knew this    the men in leadership at the church
that denied me    a bible study    leadership position
because i am a woman    preferring instead    to give
it to a lesser    equipped male    those men    never
represented    christ    the god i know    and
understand    to be true    is myriad    unable to be
contained in one gender    or identity    he is the
christ    who bears no    ill will    towards those
who would slay him    she is kali    brought forth
to conquer    a demon horde    that could not
be tamed    by man    at once    to be feared

and embraced    she is more    truly god    than any
man    i have ever known    black enough    to absorb
my darkness    i entrust her    with my care    and
she    entrusts me    to my own will    and desire
as any mother would

## sometimes still

the cold chill    of november    runs down my spine
and i have to breathe    and remember    it is all    as
it should be    though i still have    no    guarantee
no one    ever does    though i still    want    for so
much more    i have all    i need

when my heart aches    i have to remember    the
mothers    who have reason    to grieve    and trust
that they will find    peace    while i don't understand
how it all works out    i have always trusted    and it
always has    and so    i trust again    step out

and the stone    rises    saw off the limb    upon
which    i sit and find    the unaccountable ways
in which    limbs    are fastened
        *you could have driven    that car home*    the
    haitian man said    *even if it wasn't working    you're
    that powerful*

and i conjure him    in moments    when i doubt
to remind me    of what the stranger knew    that i
am able    to command these winds    of fortune
to direct this adrift bark    and arrive    on prosperous
shores    of my own    for years    i have lived    a
hand to the heavens    and nothing much

has changed    'cept the god    who comes calling
through ravens' caws    the murderous tumult    in
predawn darkness    and i look through    brightening
skies    in welcome    for i will keep    them alive
the distant gods    the strangers    come friends
who keep    me alive

## chilé verde

my people never get cancer     *it's the chilé*
mom would say     tears running down     her
flushed face     *burns away the impurities*
          *why do you eat it*     i would ask     my uncle
tony     bright red     sweating from the heat     i
watched     more than once     grandpa rolling
jalapeños in his hands
          *to get them mad*     he'd say     we all knew
this meant     to make them hotter     then he'd take
a bite     savoring     the fire     raging in his mouth
i led my aunt     to the bathroom one thanksgiving
after she got chilé     splashed in her eye     from lizzy
throwing a roll to her     across the table     it was one
of the biggest     crystal vats     of chilé verde     i've
ever seen     aunt margaret has never     had to wear
glasses     *it's the chilé*     mom would say     burned
away the impurities

# the fear that    it    defines us

*for dave chappelle's friend daphne dorman*

i'm beginning    to believe    that the worst part of
making a mistake    is the fear that    it    is all    we
will be remembered for    but i am simultaneously
realizing    if it can be lost    it was not a defining
characteristic anyway    not life    nor job    nor
relationship    none of it    is essentially    who we
are    as humans    so to the trans woman    who took
her life    jumping off that building    after being
bullied    on twitter    that is not    the story    that will
be told    or is    being told about    your precious life
i can't say i know    what was going    on in her head
or heart    that it would all just    come to naught
but i have experienced    the pain of uncertainty    i
have walked to the edge    and looked down    a time
or two    but nothing    that is going on    can replace
the promise    of tomorrow    so my prayer for that
woman is    that she wakes up    in a field of gold
having crossed over    from perceived burden    to
blessing    that her chance    to watch over her child
is multiplied    by the surrender    of her corporeal
body    and that her child    can bear the burden    of
the absence    of this parent    in such a way    that
she will be strengthened    may she rise up    and
forgive    the mother    that jumped    may she find
a way    to live

## rousing the dead

if i went    to a teller of fortunes    would you speak
to me    from beyond    or would i get    a scathing
rebuke    like saul

if i went    to a diviner of dreams    could they tell
me    how you are    so far away now    and i am
blind    cannot see

if i went    to a reader of palms    would these
broken lines    come together    to fashion
a future    and a hope

if i went    to a reader of bones    would they scatter
all and fall    or would they    tell a tale    i need
to hear

if i looked    into the tea cup    would the leaves
point me home    would they    convey a message
essential

or are these    like my dreams    just emptiness
the scattered attempts    of the desperate
to rouse the dead

## the dowager speaks

my masseuse    rather alarmed    told me for the
second visit in as many weeks    that i had the flaring
spine fins of a marlin    i lay    face down on the table
and asked    *how to do that    exercise again    shut the
gate    and open the window*    the gate    being my
shoulder blades    so i left    rather concerned

i recalled my years of yoga    and reflected inward
as my back ached    from closing the gate    and
opening the window    my chest splayed    my
anterior pelvic tilt    shifted back    spine correctly
aligned    it occurred to me    how i have fallen
into this    particular slump

the doctor's eyes met mine    as i sat    upright
back connected    to every part of the chair    after
realizing    i had slumped down again    while the iv
was being placed    the nurse set the remote    on my
lap and i said    *no thank you*    and turned myself
inward

spine erect    i remember how fiercely    i have
carried myself    through life    not hiding or
blushing    but fifty    did something to me    it was
as though the collapsible chair    of my life    refused
to stay open    and    i    folded up    on myself

inward    deeper    and deeper only those closest
to me    were allowed near    but i am also    too
determined    to accept    such a state    to allow
myself    to fold

and so i open my chest    to the back bend    of every
moment    like when i was young    and strong
though i am not old    i am just learning    how to
accept    that this body's ideas    are not always
acceptable    outward manifestations    of inward
realities    and the doctor jiggles    my bootied foot
        *you'll be fine*    he said    *you're young*

# step four

*made a searching and fearless moral inventory of*
*ourselves.*               alcoholics anonymous

i'm not a particularly    immoral person    but my
overzealous morality    has at times    created issues
where perhaps    none exist    my delicate conscience
casting myself    a criminal    for crimes    quite
possibly explained    if not understandable    at
present they center    around a pet    my four year
old    black mutt    dying in the passenger seat
beside me    fresh prescription in hand    the xrays
showed    he was    riddled with cancer    there was
     *nothing to do    except take    him home    to die*
i was a new mother    and had    no idea what to do
my one year old in a car seat    and a freshly dead dog
so i pet him    after we met eyes    he was saying
     *i waited for you*    i unclipped his collar    and
deposited him    in a ditch    where i'd watched
coyotes    and other fallen animals    meet with death
i had    no idea    this was    a bad decision    and
even now    look back in horror    at my seeming
callousness    i'm not of the pet cemetery set    and i
truly    loved that dog    but i'm sure    there were
other options    though i did not    know them    at
the time

which reminds me
of a roommate    i left without notice    and she never
mentioned the hardship    it caused her    even years
later    probably about the time    i abandoned my
dead dog    i did call her    and all i could    say was
        *i'm sorry    i was clueless*    how far    does
cluelessness    go as a justification    how have my
acts    perhaps not immoral    so much as    impolite
or improper    harmed those    closest to me    how
can i ever    make amends

## meet me

sometimes i ask if we can meet during the day
while her husband is at work    i leave my car by the
metaphysical shoppe    where we sit in the evenings
and read tarot    she calls me the sun    something
unhidden    a card pulled often    then reminds me
        *i can be a lot to take*    during the day    we lay
on the floor of her sewing room    bodies dusted
with stray blue and green thread    laughing
reading about palmistry    as we compare the whorls
on our fingers    trace the lines    on each other's
hands    when we lose track of time    i dash away
he saw    me arriving    early    one morning
mentioned it    in an email she ignored
        *i saw her    you know*    he doesn't want to hear
about me    to know i love his wife    in the way
only two women    can love    we spend entire days
laughing    reminding each other    over chicken tikka
masala    and cosmos    of who we are

*for jean*

## him or me

her hazel eyes welled up with tears
        *one of us has to die*    she said

and the waiter walked up to bring the check
        *when did i know it was over*
        *what was the last straw*
        *what made me leave my husband*

my mind wanders back through the years that have
passed    as i look at you    turning to the waiter
and smiling
    *thank you*    with red    watery eyes    and a
mustered smile

always a lady    so fierce    yet so fragile

sometimes    when i enter your home    your
turquoise bandana    folded in a triangle

holding back    your blonde hair    you open
the door    then fall onto the couch    looking up at
me    with your chin    sinking into the cream leather

your chocolate chip whippet    curled up on the
persian rug    beside you i watch    as he keeps his
eyes    locked on you

while i curl up in your chair     pull my legs up and
listen     to what ails you

       *what made me leave my husband*
       *what was the last straw*

as we left the restaurant     to run errands take
your whippet     to the vet

your words haunt me
      *one of us     has to die*

## fragile

i await their pilgrimage     the arduous journey
of the delicate monarchs     migrating  south through
my one acre     of texas cornfield     battalions of them
streaming  by     orange flares set off     by some
internal clock     some ingrained need     to mate in
deep forests     drink from     salt pools     i remember
counting them     as they waft by     carried by will
and beauty     she sits across from me     and weeps
telling me     how she's locked     into her marriage
          *trapped*     she says     *and doesn't know how
to get out*     i don't know what to say     how to tell
her it is a lie     that being trapped is all     an illusion
          *you just can't see your exit yet     but it's coming*
i leave it at that     and we find another soul     locked
in her home
          *we've been fighting*     she says     waking the
dead     she means     we sit     understanding as
women     with children     what can be done     how
to get away     from  the men     who control our lives
          *i told you     it takes courage to leave*     she said
and i begin     to understand     how can something
so fragile     so beautiful     possibly make     the
journey  alone     there is too much danger     to go
too much danger     to stay

## step five

*admitted to god, to ourselves, and to another*
*human being the exact nature of our wrongs.*
                    alcoholics anonymous

so i guess    that would be you    awkward    isn't it
hearing    the confession of  stranger    sin    is
profoundly interesting in that    one must embrace
a religious tradition    for the concept    to even apply
which i don't    and on that point    could call this
exercise    dredging for some    titillating detail
one that will both    engender disrespect at the callous
nature of    such a sin    and some curious    respect
for the very same    reason    in the buddhist
tradition    there is a    start where you're at
approach    no  come to the waters    and get clean
because cleanliness    is elusive    at best    my
greatest sin    if you can call it that    is my inability
to communicate    honestly    with my partner
some of this    i could chalk up    to being pisces
but i'm taking ownership here    how i long    to
communicate    genuinely but it seems    i do passive
aggressive    most often    she divines    what i need
because she cares    not    because    i ask for it    i'm
hard to live with    that much    i know    i don't
pretend    that i'm easy    or even accommodating
perhaps i was    once    but life    and relationship

have taught me     that if i don't     take care of myself
no one     will

                              that i force     others     to
meet     their own needs     could by some accounts
be considered     a sin     i call it     second nature

## the way of warriors

gourd dance    is danced by a warrior  society
and the men    dance alone    the women    circle the
arena    in support of these veterans    modern day
warriors    norma anquo hess    a marine    and
kiowa    taught me    the traditional dances    she
handed me her white    eagle feather fan    as we
stood    behind the men    two rows of women deep
kiowa  everywhere
        *don't drop it*    she said    a year into my life
on the powwow circuit    gourd dance became a
staple    i danced the five hour dances    praying
the entire time    feeling spirit    come through the
ground    the air    the drum    i dance for my father
vietnam    army veteran    mystery to me    i prayed
that entire year for him    and blessed his courage
when my gorgon was born    i gourd danced Jackie
to sleep    many a night    still    when i go to Denver
i meet the sun    rising over the rockies    and pray
gourd dancing    the way warriors of old    have
always done

## proximity

sometimes    those closest    use their position
to lash out    and make us bleed    to doubt our
brilliance    with words like    stupid    and to quiver
with rage    at being    disrespected

i've swallowed    my rage    many a time    justified
your behavior    though friends    tell me
        *it's abusive    the way he speaks to you*

there's always    a reason to stay    a reason    i can't
set out    on my own    by his position    he cuts me
down    attempting    to keep me    bound    by lies
that i am    still    worthless

but i know    that is    not true    you told me once
        *look in the mirror    every day    and say    i'm
desired*    and i wish    my champion    and husband
were one

## distance myself

and so    i will distance myself    from this    waking
dream    where you have left    and i am still    sitting
here    recounting in my mind    how i could have
done things differently    stubborn    as the cat    that
refuses    the tender hand    of comfort    but rather
slinks away    in line of sight    and watches    from
the perceived safety    of distance    i know this trick
when in human form past    i have used it    to see
if the hand    that threatened to hold me    intended
kindness    or if the degeneration of that    comes later
after i have given up    my heart space    and tried to
make a home    beside you    i am tentative now
these many years later    though i remember    the
tender humiliations    of loving you    the beauty
i thought    would be ours    the reality    of domestic
abuse    and trying to forget    the confines    of the
religion that bound me to you    i had to leave it all
to walk away    to preserve myself    some shred
of dignity    and here i sit    startled from sleep    still
hoping    you are well    and wishing i could kill this
caring that swirls    inside of me    but that is what
love does    changes you    forever    that is what
i thought i had found    in the church    in my
marriage    in my life    but i had been mistaken
and had to gather up    my dignity    and walk away

## the way of mares and stallions

she left him    the only time    he would let her go
at night    heavy with life    to the forest to foal
she turned her back on the band stallion
who stole her away    and held her    under watchful
eye    she stepped    one burdened    step after
another    to the ravine    a sip of water    through
the  stream    and up the side of  the mountain
she knew    he'd be there    under the cover
of darkness    she would    find him well
and waiting    her  arrival    she would labor
there with him    her stallion    the one she
watched    slip away    one hoof trod path
after another    to the edge of the timberline
she rose    certain she could    traverse
no farther    she would live or die    here in
the search    exposed    but free    she would
forge her own path    apart    under the cloak of
darkness    she trembles    the life in her
struggles    to come forth    in an explosion
of agony    and ecstasy    a trembling foal    is born

## step six

*we're entirely ready to have god remove all these*
*defects of character.*        alcoholics anonymous

as if     it were    that easy    god    as a twenty
four hour    lavandería    comforting    as that idea is
when a flooded tent    at a rainy    stanford powwow
could result in hypothermia    i've never been good
at stain removal    opting rather    to discard    or
downplay stains    rather than    try to remove them
this seems    more plausible    that god doesn't
refashion    the soldier's ear    but rather    teaches
a new way of hearing    my defects include
inhospitability    not necessarily    to those    i love
though far too often    i grow tired    of them    i
understand    when they grow tired    of me    i am
not isis inhospitable    though perhaps    a quick
death    would be preferable    to the slow burn of
cohabitation with me    my defects    or shadow
as the jungians    have helped me to understand it
will never    go away    but that    is no cause for
alarm    when i was a christian    and my shadow
reared its head    i ached and bled    for having
regressed    now i sip a cup of tea    with the
darkness    that is me    and the stains    that will
not wash out    become reminders    of where i've
been    nothing more    than a drop    of curry

or a smatter    of paella    something cherished
perhaps life giving once    memories    not soon
forgotten

# the ministry of horses

they searched me over    and let me run my hands
under their manes    around their cheekbones
down their foreheads    between their eyes    to the
tips of their noses    scratching that unreachable itch
they    because they've no hands    i    because i've
grown accustomed    to sorrow    they diligently
sniffed and explored me    with their fleshy lips
offering what my gorgon calls    *horsey kisses*
breathing    warm breath for me to breathe in
the cherokee say    *if you breathe into a horse's nostrils*
*he will never forget you*    i breathed them in today
bucky    the wild norwegian fjord    tender and tame
at my hand    a soulmate of sorts    and prince    the
black stallion    whose braided mane    was falling
into disrepair    bucky has captured my heart    and
today rested his head gently    heavily    upon my
shoulder    the entire length of my upper arm
finding the magic leather binding holding my hair
back with a stick    kokopelli hunched and dancing
he wanted to make a snack    or game out of it    but
i need this pilantir    this seeing leather    it is my
common crown    and i    am an uncommon queen
upon each arm today    they nestled close to me
a ministry of healing    from two fallen knights
who would see me    stand again    and smile

43

## teacup balrog

the prime directive when leash training a five month
young puppy    is avoid trauma    finely balanced
with    socialize your dog    to the squawking
reversing sound of an amazon truck    the squeals
of small children    the rattle of the dreaded garbage
can    these things coupled with the natural wonders
of lake living    squirrels    birds    bear    and deer
lurking in the dark woods    bordering our predawn
walks    are all fodder for fearsome encounters    if
the mind    runs away with you    like the giant dogs
some large in size    others mighty in constitution
dragging their reluctant owners    to the next
encounter    so on this latest walk    out of the inky
black night    a fearsome    snarling    eyes aglow
in my headlamp    chihuahua    emerges    from the
side of the road    my walking stick    fondly named
faun tumnus    in hand    my puppy trained to sit
beside me when stressed    sits as i wield    in Gandalf
like fashion    the bear bell bedangled    faun Tumnus
swirling the stick    and slamming it to the ground
before this demon of the night can inflict wound
or further trauma on my little    fur baby
          *NO*    rings out and the demon stops dead
in his tracks    and time obliges with a pause
crisis abated    we walk on    into the darkness

## empty of sorrow

*here anyone can begin again, but first*
*the heart must be empty of sorrow*
                    pei ti and wang wei

how i've tried    to run    the cistern dry    opened
full    the tap    of sorrow    bathed in it    scrubbed
my face arms    chest    legs    and belly    with
exfoliating sorrow    releasing    layer after layer
of who i perceived myself to be    finding a stranger
someone known    only to you    a shadow    a shade
with my face and name    the mourning of dreams
of knowing    of hope    the release of comfort
and still    there was sorrow    around every bend
vendors filled my arms    with sheaves freshly cut
the sorrow of the old woman at the crossroads    *la*
*llarona*    weeping    her children lost    picasso's
lovers    weeping    their despair    it filled my lungs
pumped through my veins    and i ceased    trying
to rid myself of it    but agreed to bear    this weight
until the debt was paid    mine or another's    until
the sorrow left of its own    and sweated out my pores
there are some days renewal    seems possible
some days    i am not a stranger    to myself some
days    sorrow is not my sole companion    and some
days
                    some days

# dusty girl

i remember the circle dance    in the dusty field
in manteca    i camped with rene navarro    an apache
fancy dancer    whose double bustle    hung    over
his waterbed    in farmersville    every weekend
i'd drive from lancaster    to wherever the biggest
local prizes    were offered    not to compete    i
never had    a coming out    was never    officially
a part of the powwow highway    but that year
1994    i spent every weekend camping    beside rene
dancing with norma    a kiowa    who was the fierce
independent    type of woman    i love    i had just
met the cousin    of a band of apaches    i had come
to know    not rene's mescalero kin — another band
san carlos    we passed on the stairs    at the
southwest indian museum    and our eyes met    i
gave him my number    and he called    fifteen years
we've been married now    i am seeking custody of
our thirteen year old    while he    is in exile in Texas
unemployed    i don't know    how i'll manage
to rent an apartment    a real one    with bedrooms
and leave the home    of the chief    of the ramapough
nation    who has let me    shelter with his family
i don't know    what the judge will say    monday at
3:30    in family court    but that one glance    the
sixteen years    it took me    to finish my bachelor's
the struggle    of single motherhood    if i could tell

that dusty girl     she would keep dancing     that it
would be all right     even the bad choices     she might
not     be so afraid     to believe

## mantras

the sweet smell of alfalfa    mixes with the smell
of ammonia    *keep the good    release the bad*
turning over each shaving of wood    my breathing
falls into a cadence    with my raking
lift    swing    release    lift    swing    release
the pile smashes against the wall    gathering up
the heavy manure    delicately sifting the clean
shavings out    turning to fill the wheelbarrow
when too tired to continue    i walk out    to bucky's
paddock    rounding the corner of the barn    he lifts
his head    sees me and turns    he approaches
the fence line    my stallion    though he is not mine
his velvet soft lips on my face    exhales i breathe him
in    and slide my hand under his mane    to scratch
he wraps his head down my back    and nuzzles
my jacket    we groom each other    for a momentary
lifetime    until i return to the next stall    and resume
sifting through the bad    and keeping the good
sifting through the bad    and keeping the good
sifting through the bad

## step seven

*humbly asked him to remove our shortcomings.*
alcoholics anonymous

it's kind of like calling   the snow plow guy
you've got   ten inches of snow   two shovels
one missing a handle   being from california
i still find   the snowfall   enjoyable   on a sunday
morning   when everyone   is home   but i know
sooner or later   i will have to extract   my car
from under   the snow pile   and  teach
                    i cannot even comprehend
how people abandon   their cars   to the sides
of unplowed roads   in clifton new jersey   the
carsicles   take up giant swaths   of parking
in paterson   entire  lanes   of the heaviest traffic
prone areas   i guess   asking god   to remove
shortcomings   is a lot   like having to figure
your way out   of the driveway   before   your car
freezes   into a carsicle   i know   i cannot do it
alone   so i hope   expectantly   that the  goodwill
of the friend with the snowplow   has not   yet
run out   this uncertainty   is a lot   like what i feel
with this whole   religious removal of sin idea
don't get me wrong   shortcomings   are sins
the painful ways   we miss the mark   day in
and day out

i have vowed    to buy    a better
shovel    salt the driveway    liberally    and to invest
in a snowblower    sooner    rather than later    i have
always    hated    being at the mercy    of someone
else

## self portrait

the witches     i have known     have not been
bedraggled and obvious     they look     and act
just like     my partner     my best friend     my gorgon
there is no self loathing     i'm sure that it makes
the steepled     feel more at ease     to imagine
the creatures of darkness     want to dwell in their
particular brand     of light     and not in the light
of bonfire     and candle     the waters are alive
not the baptismal     but the rivers     the oceans
the pools     where we swim     the feathers
and cards     are real     no doubt     but they are
not all     they are only a part     and each witch
i have known     has her specialty     some in dreams
some weather     some speak with the dead     but
none are fearful     to behold     just women     bare
of foot     and dancing     maybe a samba     or belly
dance     sometimes     they cackle     and advise
other times     they get up     go to work     and come
home     some play     the drum     meet up with their
coven     and others     are more comfortable     in the
kitchen     solitary     some are old     but most
are young     even     if they have aged

## realization

family doesn't    just happen
but it cannot    be forced
when children come together
in new families    their lost paradise
parades    on the ceiling
a projection light    of stars
only    these are not    wishing stars
aglow with promise    and delight
these are    hot coals    embers
raining down    on the old    dead wood
of marital promises    the family
that would never be    more alive
than the family    that is    how powerful
the longing    of children    for what
they imagined to be true    and we
the citizens    of pompeii    all ash
frozen in time    for others    to decipher

## teenage driver

my gorgon    is driving now    seventeen
and i let them    leave    at night    on sussex
county    winding roads    having paid for
behind the wheel training    and given them a
triple a    card

        i trust

even caught myself    making the sign
of the cross    as my grandmother did
on our foreheads    each time we left her
presence

        as my partner was driving me
home last night    a car sped by    and i knew my
gorgon    would be    setting out    on those  roads
soon    i asked the angels of mercy    to guard
them    and the hands of kindness    to  help them
i entrust them    to all the good    that kept me
foolish teenager that i was    alive until now
i exhale    as the car's headlights    fade from view
and await the sound    of their footsteps    through
the front door    announcing

       *i'm home*

# step eight

*made a list of all persons we had harmed and*
*became willing to make amends to them all.*
                    alcoholics anonymous

the *my name is earl* step    though it didn't take    his
mishaps    for me to adopt it    i am overly sensitive
to my own    sinfulness    and feel the bite    of my
own words    more    than the bitten    it is more my
challenge    to forgive    myself    than to be forgiven
by another    because i have kept    my list of
transgressed    against    short    once forgiven
has rarely meant    forgotten    by me    i still recall
the insensitive moments    of which    there are too
many to choose    shooting whipped cream    in the
face of a friend    as he drove    a truck loaded
with our friends    down a road    the pinnacle
of stupidity    some people activate    the idiot in me
and i have long    atoned for it    but now
i remember that moment    and treat myself    as i
would    my child    once restored    embraced
forgiven    let the memory    sink    into the murk
of the past    and free myself    to move    forward
for i    have always been    the one    i needed most
to make amends with    to love    and forgive
in spite    of myself

## inexplicable

i have never     pretended     to know
     seems now     even less
          certain only     of all     i cannot understand
          i send blessings     from afar
tender hand     at times     inexplicably immature
     harsh words     you learned     to dodge
so many wonderful experiences     we've shared
     mothers are never meant to be friends
     we are just grateful     when it happens
          we just rejoice     at the growth
          the wonder     the mystery
of time unfolding     holding close
          these young souls     gifted
     to us     from some     place in time
          hoping to make it right
     past lives' grievances     revisited
          upon us     why else could you
     be     so angry     with me
               we carry     our yesterdays
     into tomorrow
               and i wish you well
                    today my love
                         i wish you well

# bewitching

*the skin of a real witch makes a delicate binding for*
*a book of common prayer.*     elizabeth willis

it has been the fortune     of powerful women
to be feared     and persecuted for their     strengths
to sever one breast     to draw the bow     more nearly
to house     the healing     and slaying blood
of gorgons     the remedy     for men's ailments
and excuse for the execution     yet when the woman
is tamed she     is hailed     in her beheaded state
as goddess     powerful even in death

i say     *let her live*     the poster on the women's
bathroom stall     reads     *he makes me feel worthless*
and i think     *then dump him     no one can     make you*
*do anything*     the campaign for emotional strength
writings on the mirror     *look at how lovely you are*
again     seeing only     the exterior     the shell
a woman's mind     is  housed in

they feared her     but in death     she grew stronger
her face had the power     to turn     men to stone
they emblazoned her     on the shields of kings
and she     gorgon ruler     slithers through my home
naga kanya     the protector     and i come to her now
dare to gaze     into obsidian eyes     and ask her

to guard    my gorgon    her patron    the one
who understands    her power

*why don't they remind them    they have brains*
*and the power    to use them    instead    of focusing*
*on the externals*    why are women    still unable
to walk alone    through crowded cities    without
being harassed    by some    ne'er do well    so i
conjure them    and ask    the serpents    of old
the goddesses    of the past    to guard them

they understand    my request    having daughters
and sisters    mothers    and wives    of their own
they rouse me    from my sleep    to join them
in their battle    my grams    who dwells    on the
other side    she goes before and behind    she is
everywhere    and nowhere    seen    and unseen
she stands with kali    and    quan yin

and i    drift back to sleep    and trust    they will
guide them

# lament

*she lived in solitude,*
*and now in solitude*
*has built her nest;*
*and in solitude he guides her,*
*he alone, who also bears*
*in solitude the wound of love.*

st. john of the cross

here then is my
source of grief
i, love starved
cannot feast

here then is my
source of woe
i, mortally wounded
cannot die

here then is my
source of shame
i, broken wife
cannot bear

here then is my
source of pain
i, half alive
cannot live

## step nine

*made direct amends to such people wherever*
*possible, except when to do so would injure them*
*or others.*               alcoholics anonymous

it is hard    this step    to make amends    because
one must    release the guilt    of offense committed
but also    the need to see    the wrongdoer    suffer
this morning    we awoke    to a crash    raced up
the stairs    to find a toppled birdcage    and the
parakeets    beneath the separation grate    their finch
counterparts    ominously    silent    door open to the
cage beside    i looked into their nesting box    and
ran    upstairs    to find the sweet    meticulously
clean brothers    one strewn this way    and the other
that    i forgot    to double latch    the cage    after
cleaning it    yesterday    and the saffron eyed
grey kitten    made use of the night hours    and
opportunity to do    *what cats do*    the silence in the
house    is oppressive    the brothers    laid out
in a spent    valentine's candy box    filled with rose
petals    and i am so sorry    for what    i    have not
done    my partner says    *you cannot blame a cat*
*for killing*    i realize    i can accept    all blame
for though i was    and am    perpetually distracted
it was my oversight    that killed the sweet finches
how do i begin to forgive    myself    the cat
           myself    for hating    the cat

59

## that woman

i don't want to be    that woman
who falls in love    with charlie
manson    because    there is
something    about    his eyes

i don't want to be    that woman
whose    vengeful    shih tzu
ling ling    dispatches    directives
to    david    berkowitz

i don't want to be    that woman
who shacks up    with ted
kazinsky    and goes for
sunday drives

 i don't want to be    that woman
who gives    head
to richard    ramirez
after    she dies

i don't want to be    that woman
who wants to share    with jeffrey
dahmer    her culinary secrets
and    japanese knives

# the masseuse

i love the strong    nimble fingers    of asian women
the ache    as she rubs my shoulders    the glide
of her hands    through the oil
         *is this okay    more gentle    you can tell me*
she says softly    her hands    are like vise grips
my instinct to scream    but i breathe in    deeply
as she works the knot    out of my shoulder
         *this hurt yes*
         my second visit    in as many weeks    she
locked her thumb    between my toes    and
massaged crystal gel    up my calves    to my knee
cap    sometimes    i just need touch    the manicurist
holds my hand    while i relax    and try not    to
hold back    to leave palms open    to receive    they
are not there    for the same reasons as i    perhaps
but when she rubbed my back    down to my hips
after the manicure    i made a second appointment
she worked my lower back    long and hard
because she knew i stand all day    naked    all i could
think of    was how    i would do this for you    as
soon as possible    she jumped on the table    side
saddle    our hips touching    and leaned her weight
on my ass    bracing herself    palm open    against
my left cheek    as she worked    my back    i melted
into the massage table    and blessed her    strong
hands    her unabashed silence    the touch that
grounds

## khaos

pushing the mower up the hill    i wonder when
i swore myself    into your service    this    spartan
year    of digging out    and i keep asking    why
is the theme    of khaos    repeating

the cage door open    grabbing bowls of wild finch
food    when one buzzes my head    our tabby kali
leaps up on the counter    eager    for a challenge
the zebra finch    sits atop the cabinet    panting
and i scoop up    the tabby

the frog hops from the grass    before the mower
i stop and search him out    when playing chicken
with a frog    or turtle in the road    they must be
allowed the chance    to win    and so i push    the
mower    elsewhere

my style of organization    is to create    khaos first
then restore order    each day    khaos first    then
order    and i see this theme    weaving through my
life    i try to trace    the origins back    when did i
ally myself    to khaos

when did primordia    become such a part of my life
i embrace    the creative power of destruction    but
not today    and scoop up    the russian blue    who

hasn't had a finch challenge    in years    and lob him
into the bathroom    with kali

i circle the kitchen a few times    and have no idea
where the net is    this being    not my first    finch
wrangling    unfound    i grab a blanket    as the
poof of feathers    indicate a ferrel    finch landing
i scoop    him up
        *this is how you die*    i say

and the calico    who was my companion    for ten
years    would walk with me    to yoga    wait in the
bushes    until i emerged    then follow me    to the
river    where i accidentally    dropped him in    like
a cork    or jesus    popped up    then sat beside me
bankside

must be allowed    to offer himself    to death    who
had come knocking    i held him    on my lap
begging    for forgiveness    he never    wanted to be
indoors
        *i am so sorry    i didn't know*    i said    *i am so
sorry greggy*    how i miss him now

the finch's heart beats fast    i unfurl my hand in the
cage
        *there you are safe*

63

and she     is here     beside me     safe     because
the debt     was paid     my gorgon     goes off to live
with a tabby     of their own     and i know     this is
how it works

khaos first     then order     i let the cats     out of the
bathroom     but kali is revisiting     everywhere
the finch was     and i try to tell her     he is safe
khaos will come again     but not today

## kissing cobras

the burmese snake priestess
must kiss the king cobra
three times to summon rain
for her people

the end of a weekend together
our insecurities clash   and i try
to avoid the argument i know
is coming

the sepia film flickers as she
draws her ankle length cotton
dress up and squats down to look
into the cobra's eyes

*i'm so uncomfortable*
you say   after my silence has
eroded the last   of your
patience   i knew it was coming
but i tried to   stave it off

the cobra rears up half his
length his black hood flared
his head moving slowly
side to side   his tongue
tastes the air

*then leave*    i said
the first few words    i manage
after closing    you out
isolating you    with silence
i knew    it would come to this

                    the priestess sways side
                    to side matching the
                    cobra's rhythm and she
                    leans over him and
                    kisses him on the head
                    then pulls away

*this is my house*    furious
now    and raging    you could
say i pushed you there    that i
made you angry    though i tried
to remind you    some people
fight    when they part

                    the cobra still swaying    tongue
                    flickering    seems in a  daze
                    from the first kiss    when she
                    kisses him again    right on the
                    head

*listen*   you say
and i know what's coming
how you will tell me you
don't love me    though i know
you do    i know you do

        the priestess shrinks
        back into a seated squat
        as the cobra lunges      she
        reaches out    two fingers
        touch his abdomen    below
        the hood    gentle pressure
        but enough      to stave off a
        bite      he strikes again

and i listen     in tears now to
you tell me    *we're not right*
*for each other*    then pull out
of your boston driveway
headed home

        the priestess leaps back
        the strike hits her outer
        garment    a long apron
        that keeps the venom
        filled fangs from reaching
        their target

i drive away and

realize     it may be over
or it may     just be
another leg of our journey

                    she rights herself and sways
                    toward him     the cobra
                    reared up     eyeing her with
                    cool indifference     and she
                    reaches out     one more time
                    and kisses his head

we talk later that night
        *i'm still here     i still love you*
and you begin to realize
you love me

## and be eaten

                         at low tide
walking down nantasket beach
the clams    half buried    still
alive    though hordes of gulls
mine their quarry    i drew one
of these clams    out of its
sheltering hole    and tossed it
back to sea    the white fleshy
tongue    of the handless clam
elongates    and digs into the
sandy bottom    the next clam
i pick up    slightly opens in my
hand    the hairy edge of the shell
pulsing    as the labia begin
to separate    and i see the tongue
inside    wet tenuous    my aggressive
tongue    leads the charge down
the shore    to the kelp beds    and
nestles in    the kelp on the beach
held clams in a moderate moisture
and scant protection from the gulls
i watched the gulls    pick up a clam
fly ten feet up    then drop it
cracking open the shell
drawing out the flesh    with a prying
beak    my tongue circles in your
tidepools    then plunges in

headlong     to feel the arch
of your back     the clamoring
of hands     deeper     pulling in
to drink you     feel you contract
and i toss the clam to sea
harboring no ill will     toward
the gulls for i know     everyone
      must eat

## step ten

*continued to take personal inventory and when
we were wrong promptly admitted it.*
                              alcoholics anonymous

here's the thing about amends    you have to want
the suffering    to stop    as i walked    by my
bookshelf    after lighting    nag champa    goldberg's
*the great failure*    caught my eye    call it my flair
for the dramatic    or just a human soul    in search
of relief    either way    i am profoundly aware
of all my shortcomings    at the moment    my gorgon
counts the number    of pets    i have
            *killed*    they say    of course any number
is heartbreaking    but the loss of the finches
makes me wonder    if i shouldn't just    open a
slaughterhouse    and butcher cows    for a living
blood soaked    brain splattered clothes    there's
some honesty there    i have seen many creatures
through the portal    to the next life    and consider
it my call    of sorts    from the ailing butterfly
going still on my chest    to the cancer ridden dogs
i have known    their souls    and mine    intersect
my grief for them    perhaps    not outward    in the
monument erecting manner    but more    the bury
them    beneath a bed    of oriental lilies variety
i have to help    the suffering stop    theirs    and

my own    how kevorkian that sounds    death
has taught me    how to hold on    with an open
hand    and to let    life    evolve    the spirit world
more real    than this    atom    and energy dream
we inhabit    but i never    can get used to
the profound silence    the somebody    say
something    goddammit    silence    after
a death

# fear period

*for suki moon paws*

my ten month young puppy    is going through
what experts call    a fear period    a time when
dogs need exposure    to various sights    and
sounds    experiences    to help them    gain
confidence    when their wiring    is screaming
run    or worse    cower

my fear period began    at fifty    i would like to
think it is ending    that i have reckoned with
my rabid thoughts    as effectively as possible
and wrangled them into some form    of wisdom
something like today    at the car wash

my fur baby    buckled into the passenger's seat
as i eased the car    into the stall    slowly so
the undercarriage wash can remove    some of the
metal eroding brine    that coats    nj highways
and devours    undercarriages    my pup

was inconsolable    the last time    i drove through
the wash with her    as the giant blue spinny
things    and gobs of white foam    dolloped on my
car    she gasped    not really    but that is how it
felt    and i pulled her close to me    held her

in my arms    as i felt her tremble    when the brushes
whooshed over the top of my car    she watched the
spindly brushes    down the back window    and
trembled

again as they made their return    her body not
cold    but the fear    run straight through her
and i held her tight    and told her    *we've made
it*    when the brushes tucked back in    like a
plane's landing gear    and we eased out of the

chamber of torment    that it never was    but
she didn't know that    just like i didn't know
how fifty one    would be even harder than fifty
and i would have to fight    the deep trembling
of my mind    images of what could    go wrong

had i not practiced    what could    go right
enough    did i not know better than to dwell
on darkness    but i could not step away from
these certain crevasses    and my partner
was all that could pull me back    at times

her hand on my head    working her energy
to calm me    and set me free    from what i
now understand    to be my own    fear
devising a way    to undo    all that had been
established    these many years    ago

## p.c.e.s

elevated states of
    meditation include
    pure consciousness
        experiences (p.c.e.s)
    of the unaccountable
        loss of time
the contentless presence
    of deep meditation
when floating in
    a sensory deprivation
        tank
    or undergoing
        extensive tattoo
        work
kevin    my artist
    is a philosophical
        ink master
    who approaches his
craft    with complete
    upright posture
    rivaling    any finishing
    school girl
        and such delicate
precision that i
    have had p.c.e.s under

his gun
i open my eyes and say
    *kevin when someone*
*like me comes to you*
    *and asks    can i take it?*
he smiles and says    *yeah*
    and keeps detailing
        my inner bicep
*please say this to*
    *them*
*there are other*
    *less painful locations*
        *to consider*
*will you do that for me?*
he smiles and says
    *pain should not be*
        *a factor in a permanent*
            *decision*
 i close my eyes
    and say
    *this fucking hurts*
i repeat to myself   as the
    needle bites into my skin
    *i can stop this pain at*
        *any moment*
    *with just one word*
*some people cannot*
    *escape their pain*
i inhale and exhale

i sink deeper into
　　myself and
　　　try to last
　　just one minute
　　　　more


other times　an hour
　　has passed and
　　　the razor
　　　slicing　me feels
like the gentle
　　brush of fingers
　　　across my skin
*this is crazy*
　　　i tell kevin
who agrees some of
　　his most contemplative
moments have been
　　under needle


to riff on dolly parton
　　in steel magnolias
　　　*god don't care how*
　*you get there darlin'*
　　*as long as you*
　　　*show up*

# who's calling who naive

since my separation    i have spoken to my mom
at least once a week    many weeks    almost every
day    she and i    talk about    everything    because
i would not allow her close    unless she accepted
all of me    so her    baby boomer republican Christian
perspective    does not always mesh with    my
neopagan    homosexuality    but mom has always
surprised me    i remember when    she was in the
academy    jogging    switch blade in hand    she was
fierce    though naive    or so i thought    when we
speak of it now    and i tell her    how glad i am
        *they didn't allow her into sworn duty*    because
she was    five seconds    past the cutoff    she tells me
they called her    *grandma*    at thirty six    the oldest
woman    in the sheriff's academy    which had just
begun accepting    females    i am shocked to hear
when i tell her    *i'm glad you didn't have to see all that*
*ugliness*    she chuckled on the line    and began to
describe her thirty year career    as an evidence
custodian
        *what did you think i did*    she finally asks
she tells me    how she    *laid bloody sheets out in the*
*locker room and examined    crime scene photos*
my mom    my fragile    delicate    fierce
determined mom

## reading tarot

it was a zombie oktoberfest    bands were playing all
day    i was reading tarot    publicly    for the first
time    dressed like gypsies    using the celtic cross
and one of my patrons    was an iraq veteran    he was
blonde    strong of body    stern of face    he shuffled
my thoth deck    and i laid the cards out    in the
ninth position    his hopes and fears    a rider sword
erect    in each hand    glistening armor    horse full
stride    sparrows trailing    contrail clouds spreading
through the skies    in escort    he looked at the cards
with his pale    blue eyes    then gazed at me    as i
recounted    what i believed to be    his hope    and
his fear

      *redeployment*    his face flushed red    and he
stared    wide-eyed at me    i met his gaze and said
      *you feel guilty for being home    but you have done
your duty it's time to be home*    he teared up    slightly
and i looked at the card again
      *you have served your country well and want to be
beside your brothers    that is a hope    but also you fear
not returning*    my eyes welled up    and i told him
      *you have    much to do    here    at home    be home*
we hugged    and my next client arrived    some
minutes later    escorted by the soldier    saying
      *he said    you changed    his life*
then the soldier    walked away

## step eleven

*sought through prayer and meditation to improve*
*our conscious contact with god as we understood*
*him, praying only for knowledge of his will for us*
*and the power to carry that out.*

alcoholics anonymous

as much as i try    not to attribute    ill will    to god
i try also    not to consider    all good will    only
god    both seem to    deprive man    of any credit
or fault    as the case may be    and i have found
my key    to liberation    not behind the skirts
of god    but in the naked    truth    prayer    is not
so much    my one size    fits all    answer    to
whatever    may be plaguing me    but a moment
when i commune    meditation    not the answer
to any problem in itself    but key    to the liberation
of my mind    from the hamster wheel    of mundane
concerns    i am still aware of god    even when    i
do not    attribute    every    jot    and tiddle    to her
i am still aware    that there is    a greater good
even when    i am not    busily    about    the
business    of maintaining that connection    god
unlike the hip kids    in the hallways    of school
does not    depend    on my homage    and i trust
no more    wants me to consciously    utter
            *bless this    and that*    any more    than i want

my child to remain    wholly dependent    on me
at some point    they must set off    and chart their
own course    i will always    love and support them
whether they    acknowledge it    or not    so too
god has    never needed    my praise    and
concentration    but loves me    just the same

## deadbeat

it is 7:49    at 8 o'clock
the child support enforcement
office opens    and i will call to
determine what can be done
what can i do    friends advise
        *act desperate*    while i am
in need of money    i am not desperate
no amount of acting    can make me
appear that way
        *you're mr magoo*    my best
friend says    because things
always work out    and i keep
moving forward    but when
my gorgon asks me for some
thing    and i have to tell them
        *not now    i don't have any money*
it is not a reflection    of our poverty
for we are not poor    no lack of funds
could make us poor    but we are
in need of making sound    financial
decisions    they are learning to save
to keep something    set aside to loan
to me    when the bills    consume
everything    i always repay them
with interest    this makes it
worth their while    and since

i do not believe     allowance
falls from the sky     simply
for being     i insist they earn
their allowance     they opt
only to earn interest     their
choice     so while their dad
seeks out another job
and i stretch a dollar     into
twelve it seems     this would
somehow define me     but it
does not     i am more than
my a.g.i.     we learn the value
of simplicity     lavish
ourselves in love

## the rape of a soul

having lost my mother    to stupidity    she is still
alive    but i refuse to dignify    more garbage
spewed    from a pulpit    by even listening to it

by it    i mean    to her    and so i have pulled out
all the old mothers    and these    my spiritual
mothers    marion woodman

clarissa pinkola estés    these women    who have
helped me    to find    my feminine power    their
voices reframed    my world view    at a time

when i was    subjugated    ridiculed    dominated
and dumb enough    to call that    a Christian
marriage    now i will have    none of either

christianity    or marriage    and have tried    to pull
the sullied    image of christ    from the dung heap
of man's interpretation    and reconcile

the christ    i thought i knew    with the christ
i actually received    from pulpit    from husband
from my biological mother    she would see our

division as being foretold    for it was written
        *brother shall come against brother*    and so by
extension    we were destined    by the annals of

some fucked up religion    to be at odds    except that
our dispute    arose from a political discussion
and the refrain

        *he's an idiot mom*    which she would not hear
and she called herself    *a woman of faith*    and i held
my heart in my hand    and walked away    to my

other mothers    the ones    who helped
me heal    after husband    church    had their
way with me

# the maloika

to the man at the laundromat    who in spite of my
ear plugs    and blocking    the view between us
interjected his bullshit    into my life    by saying
     *if you have a crash    in that car    you're done*
i replied
     *thank you    for the curse    but i don't receive it*

and the woman    approaching    finger extended
ready to poke out    kali's third eye    as if she could
i stepped back    in unison    with each step closer
because i have been poked    once already    by a
coworker    who bore down on me    while i was
seated at a desk    bacitracin shine    on my freshly

inked    quarter sleeve    and he stretched out    his
finger    while i watched in disbelief    that anyone
would poke a fresh wound    and i asked him
     *why would you do that*
and he replied
     *i don't know*

then wandered away    to poke some other
unsuspecting soul    i don't get it    why people insist
on hoisting    their ignorance    upon others
i'm sure i have done it    once    when in cahoots
with the religious right    i asked a question    of a
worship leader    fresh off the stage

he was so offended     and saw me     from there on
as an instrument     of the devil     i never intended
that     perhaps neither did they

and the only maloika     that has     any power
is the one     we give     ourselves     permission to
receive     and accepting the curse     play it out     to
fruition     manifest it     in consciousness     we are
far     more powerful     than we may     believe

## how benny hill saved my marriage

it was a familiar scenario    we were locked in the old
patterns    you can move    and still    take it with
you but when the couch arrived    ikea style    we
needed to assemble it    and she said
      *read the directions*    then proceeded to assemble
it    without the directions    so i said
      *wait    what*
and she said
      *really    i assemble shit    for a living*
i walked away    made coffee    and did the dishes
checked on her progress    then she needed me to
hold the couch    imagine me    half bent after weeks
of packing    and unpacking    back aching and i was
breathing heavy    trying to    hold the shit still    it is
hard to work together    we have different styles
and i am easily distracted    so later    when the couch
was built    and i was all sullen    from the experience
we could not agree    i read how to take the sting
from a memory    to suck the venom    from the
experience    by feeling    the pain of it    then playing
a song    contrary to that feeling    but in this case    i
had to speed it up    i played    the theme to benny hill
in my mind    and saw us pointing    and me grabbing
my lower back    darting around the couch    which
was inverted    on the floor    imagine the scene    in
fast forward    with the benny hill theme    dubbed
over it    how can anyone    stay mad    after that

## step twelve

*having had a spiritual awakening as the result*
*of these steps, we tried to carry this message to*
*alcoholics, and to practice these principles in*
*all our affairs.*          alcoholics anonymous

the message i carry is      *mind    the power    of intent*
each day at work    i see it    kids who are certain of
failure    and fail they do    because they convinced
themselves    they cannot succeed    each semester
much time was devoted to the power of the mind    in
higher ed    the content is largely instructor directed
i make them think    about what they want    about
where they are going    about how they will get there
not to lock them    into any decision at such a young
age    at twenty i was still lost    but to help them to
see    from a higher vantage point    what the future
could hold    and i tell them
          *your mind will help you achieve      whatever you*
*focus upon    tell yourself you will fail    your mind will*
*help you fail    tell yourself you will succeed    your mind*
*will    work out ways of helping    ensure that outcome*
it is not    all dependent    on what we choose to
believe at any particular moment    there are forces in
this world    which may    or may not    have an
impact    but i choose    to see the good in life    the
value in people    the joy of simple acts    to empower
my students    beyond the mundane

## best intentions

i meant to be     agreeable
to offer     myself up     as caviar
scraped     across     a crostini
or shrimp     doused     in cocktail
sauce     but i've become     viper
     stealthily     stalking
biting ankles     and slithering
away     to yoga     or my prayer
cushion     no different     than
when i was     a hypocritical
christian     who always
meant well     but found     herself
familiar     with     the words of
repentance
     *forgive me mother*
*for i have no clue     how*
*to be kind     or to tolerate*
*other people's children*
 — i barely tolerate my own
and they handle me sparingly
preferring to leave offerings
of silence and     space —
my partner does not     yet know
this trick and when     i find myself
lashing out     and biting kicking
and spilling her best     intentions
as if overwatering     the container

garden     and the life
giving water     overflows
onto the aged floorboards
of the porch     the flowers
languish     i turn away
and sometimes settle
into a calm     that only lasts
a day     a week     an hour
and we're all praying
i would get  my period
so i can be        irritated
by something else
the inconvenience
the white skirt     the
unchecked      flow

## this poem sucks

it's the one where my wife plays
plecostomus     our tiny ten gallon
bed and she     all mouth

the way she draws     the ocean's
flow from me     the humpback whale
rises blowhole  cleared     as she dives

deeper     the pearls she finds     and
tongues them clean     her mouth
an oval of undulating tongue     and cling

the vast     vast     valley     each ridge
tongued and turned     to the rhythmic
pulsing     of her driving

her diving
            deeper

## holy antiphon

kneel you   at
the doors      of longing

mouthing     holy antiphon
drink you    wine

eat you    bread
mouthing   holy antiphon

o' you doors    of longing open
bring you    seed of promise    come

mouth you    holy antiphon
kneel you    at the doors

of longing    mouth you
    holy antiphon

## reverse darwinism

*make a law so that the spine remembers wings*
                    larry levis

and upon remembering     forgets the terrestrial
the earthbound existence     we have come to know
let the soul again     take flight     and the bear
will come     and rummage through remains
of what was     claws tearing     and we     will lift off
toward     the silver moon     at once free     and set
right again

let the spine remember     the dorsal fin     it once
absorbed into     a calcium shield     against the
pressures     of terrain     the flippered     feet and
hands     splayed out     to cover the greatest breadths
of ocean     to mate in the warm california flow
en route to the playgrounds of summer     to breach
to birth     to nurse

let the memory of primordial ooze     the gelatinous
phase of being     before spine     before the
complicated dance     of time     and being     the
amoebic budding     and flagellum     whipping
through     the indistinguishable muck     before
cell phones     and mortgage payments

## acknowledgements

**calling back the sun, solstice mfa anthology,** 2014
> this poem sucks

**paterson literary review #42,** july 2015,
**allen ginsberg poetry prize honorable mention**
> chilé verde

**paterson literary review #41,** july 2014
> bury me in the lake
>
> step one

**stone canoe #7,** january 2013
> fragile
>
> sangre de dios

**stalking the dead,** january 2008
> a young bride
>
> calle muerto
>
> dusty girl
>
> empty of sorrow
>
> mantras
>
> the last fight
>
> the ministry of horses
>
> the way of warriors
>
> him or me
>
> meet me